This book belongs to:

_____

BRIMAX

CONTENTS

Published in Great Britain by Brimax,
An imprint of Autumn Publishing Group
Appledram Barns, Chichester, PO20 7EQ
Published in the US by Byeway Books Inc,
Lenexa KS 66219 Tel 866.4BYEWAY
www.byewaybooks.com
© 2004 Autumn Publishing Ltd
Printed in China

ISBN 1-85854-970-1

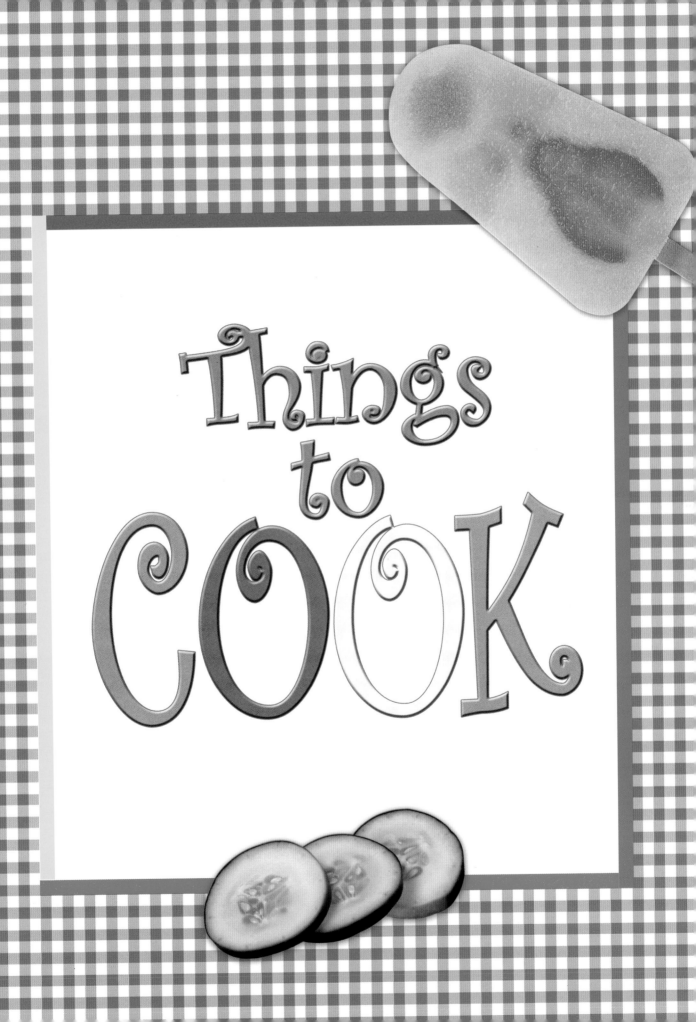

Things to COOK

How to be a Cook

Think of the lovely smells which come from the kitchen at mealtimes. Think how delicious your favourite food is. Cooking your own food is great fun.

You will discover lots of exciting new smells and tastes, and you will be very proud when you can say 'I made it myself!'

Find out how you can be a cook

Read all the instructions before you start a recipe. Follow each step carefully and ask an adult to help you whenever you see this sign ★.

Good cooks always get everything ready before they begin. That way they work faster and eat sooner!

Good cooks are clean and tidy cooks. Before you start to cook always wash your hands. Wear an apron. When you finish cooking wash up all your equipment and put everything away.

Are you ready to be a cook?

Dippy Dip

This dip tastes just as good as it looks.
Cut a carrot into pretty shapes to dip in.

You will need

1 large tomato

4 tablespoons cream cheese

½ cucumber

1 carrot, washed and peeled

1 teaspoon chopped chives

salt and pepper

Equipment

round-bladed
knife

spoon

small
mixing bowl

chopping board

small
biscuit cutters

1 Cut the top off the tomato and keep it as a lid. Scoop out the inside of the tomato with a spoon.

2 Put the cream cheese in your bowl. Chop up the inside of the tomato and the cucumber into small pieces then mix them into the cream cheese. Add the chives, salt and pepper.

3 Spoon the mixture into the tomato. Carefully cut the carrot into 5cm/2in lengths. Cut the lengths into thin slices. Cut different shapes with the cutters.

Funny Faces

Try making funny faces from fruit or vegetables. Cut up different kinds with your friends – slices and segments, lots of shapes. See who can make the funniest face.

You will need
Fruit, such as apples, oranges, lemons, pears, grapes, bananas, vegetables, such as tomatoes, carrots, cress, celery, mushrooms, cauliflower.

Equipment

round-bladed knife

chopping board   serving plate

1 Wash the fruit and vegetables you want to use, before cutting them up.

2 Prepare the fruit and vegetables, peeling if necessary. Cut very carefully into slices or separate into segments.

3 Choose the segments and slices you want to make your face.

How to cut slices

1. Always hold a knife by its handle. Make sure the cutting edge is facing down.

2. Hold the fruit or vegetables steady with one hand while you cut with the other.

3. Mind your fingers – check they are not near the blade of the knife.

4 When the faces are finished, they can be served with yoghurt for fruit faces or mayonnaise for vegetables.

Sandwich House

Make some sandwiches with your favourite fillings. Cut them into different shapes and build a house for tea.

You will need

6 slices brown bread
4 slices white bread
soft margarine
sandwich filling

Equipment

round-bladed knife

chopping
board

plate

How to spread

When you are spreading, don't press too hard or the bread will break.

How to cut off crusts

Hold the bread steady with one hand and cut away the crusts along one side with the other hand.

Turn the bread around as you cut the crust off each side.
Mind your fingers.

Choose your favourite filling –
cucumber, tomato, cheese, lettuce,
banana, peanut butter. Make 3 brown
sandwiches and 2 white sandwiches,
spreading the margarine and filling
carefully. Cut the crusts off the
sandwiches.

1 ▸ Cut one sandwich into 3 and put the
strips on top of each other.

2 ▸ Cut a white sandwich and a brown
sandwich into 9 squares each.

3 ▸ Finally put the roof on – cut 2 more
sandwiches in half to make 3 triangles
to fit the top of the house.

Cup Cakes

Cup cakes are so easy to make. Weigh two eggs and use the same weight of flour, margarine and sugar. Mix them together then put the mixture in pretty paper cases. They will cook very quickly.

You will need

2 eggs

caster sugar

soft margarine

self-raising flour

★ adult help

Equipment

scales

wooden spoon

teaspoon

paper cases

small bowl

mixing bowl

patty tins

Get everything you need ready before you begin. The oven should be switched on to 180C/350F/Gas 4.
Makes about 16.

1 Weigh your eggs. If the two eggs weigh 100 grams (4oz) you will need the same weight each of margarine, sugar and flour.

How to crack an egg

1. Tap the egg on the side of a bowl so that a crack appears on the shell.

2. Put your thumbs on either side of the crack and gently pull the shell apart so the egg slides out into the bowl.

2 Cream the margarine and sugar together in the bowl until it is light and fluffy.

4 Put a spoonful of mixture into each case.
★ Cook the cakes in the oven for about 15 minutes.

3 Add the eggs to the mixture with the flour, a little of each at a time. Mix well.

5 When the cakes are cooked, leave them to cool on a wire rack.

Icing Cup Cakes

Have some fun with your cup cakes. With coloured icing and sweets you can turn them into funny animals.

You will need

lots of cup cakes (see page 10)

100g (4oz) soft margarine or butter

250g (8oz) icing sugar

a variety of food colouring

assorted sweets

Equipment

scales

mixing bowl

wooden spoon

mug

round-bladed knife

sieve

metal spoons

several small bowls

Making the butter icing

Can you have a go now?

1 Put the margarine or butter in a very large mixing bowl. Sieve the icing sugar, a little at a time, mixing all the time. Continue beating the mixture until it is smooth and has no lumps.

The green is wonderful.

2 Divide the mixture up into several small bowls then add a few drops of food colouring to each bowl. Mix in each colour with a metal spoon.

Hints and tips for icing

1. Use metal spoons to mix in the colour, as wooden spoons will stain.

2. Brush off all the crumbs from the cakes before you start to ice.

3. Fill a mug full of warm water and dip a knife into it to help smooth out the icing.

The dragon

Cut 4 cup cakes across, making smaller slices each time. Cover in green icing and position on a plate. Make scales from chocolate wafer mints. Cut slots for the scales. Make a tongue from liquorice and eyes and feet from orange and other coloured smarties.

The mouse

Cut 1 cup cake in half. Trim one end to make a nose. Cover with pink icing. Use smarties for the eyes and slice a marshmallow for the ears. Liquorice makes a tail and spaghetti the whiskers.

The frog

Cut a cup cake across the centre, but do not cut completely through, to make a mouth. Cover in green icing, add two sweets for eyes, two for the legs and another for the mouth.

The ladybird

Cut off the top of the cup cake and then cut the top in two to make the two wings. Cover the cake and the wings in red icing. Put the wings in place. Decorate with small pieces of liquorice and use smarties for the eyes.

The pig

Cover the top of a cup cake with pink icing. Use scissors to cut a marshmallow into a small circle for the nose. Cut triangle sweets for ears. Add dolly mixture eyes and a red liquorice tail.

Magic Meringues

These pretty meringues taste as good as they look. Make some as presents or for a birthday party tea.

You will need

3 eggs
pinch of salt
150g (6oz) caster sugar
edible coloured cake balls
food colouring (if you like)
★ adult help

Get everything ready before you begin. Take out the eggs from the fridge, line the trays with paper and make sure the bowl is clean and dry. ★Set the oven to low, 75C/150F/Gas 1/2.
Makes about 36.

Equipment

saucer

cup

big bowl

small bowl

scales

electric beater/ rotary whisk

teaspoon

baking tray

silicone paper

Crack the eggs and separate the whites from the yolks. Put the whites in the large mixing bowl, add a pinch of salt and a few drops of food colouring if using. ★Whisk until whites are light and fluffy.

3 Drop teaspoons of the mixture on to the baking tray, spaced well apart.

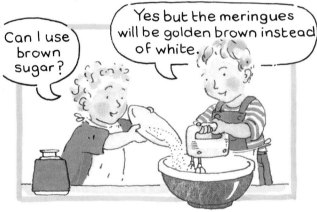

★ Add the sugar slowly to the egg whites, beating slowly all the time. Continue beating until the mixture is thick and shiny.

4 Sprinkle over the coloured balls. ★Cook in the oven for 2 hours. ★Turn off the heat and leave to cool in the oven for a while.

How to separate an egg

1. Crack the egg gently into a saucer.

2. Cover the yolk with a cup.

3. Gently tip the white into the large mixing bowl, holding the yolk in place with the cup.

Mini Pizzas

Pizzas smell so good as they cook. Make some funny face mini pizzas to share with your friends.

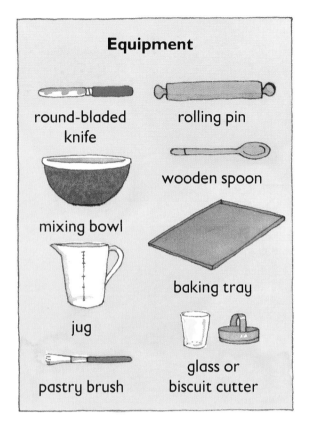

Equipment

round-bladed knife

rolling pin

mixing bowl

wooden spoon

jug

baking tray

pastry brush

glass or biscuit cutter

You will need
145g (5½oz) packet pizza dough mix
flour
oil
2 tablespoons tomato ketchup or purée
4 tomatoes, sliced
green and red peppers, seeded and sliced
100g (4oz) grated Cheddar cheese
dried oregano or mixed herbs
stoned black olives
salt and pepper
★ adult help

Weigh all the ingredients before you begin. ★ The oven should be switched on to 220C/425F/Gas 7, after you have made the dough. Oil the baking trays. **Makes 6 pizzas.**

My dough's getting thicker.

1 Empty the packet of pizza mix into a bowl and add 200ml (7fl.oz) of hand-hot water. Mix to a dough.

2 When it is all mixed in, take the dough out of the bowl, shape into a ball and knead for about 10 minutes until it is stretchy and shiny.

3 ★Turn on the oven. Sprinkle a little flour onto your work surface and roll out the dough. Use a glass or biscuit cutter to cut out circles and put them on the baking tray.

4 Brush the pizzas with oil and spread with ketchup or purée. Sprinkle over the herbs, salt and pepper. Make funny faces with the tomatoes, peppers, cheese and olives. ★Cook for 12-15 minutes.

Fast Pizzas

If you are in a hurry, you can use crumpets or muffins as the base for the mini pizzas instead of the dough mix.

Spice Bunnies

Make some little bunnies sitting on grass.
★ Turn on the oven to 180C/350F/Gas 4.
Makes about 12 bunnies and 4 bases.

You will need

250g (8oz) self raising flour
1 teaspoon ground ginger
1 teaspoon ground cinnamon
50g (2oz) margarine
100g (4oz) soft brown sugar

2 tablespoons golden syrup
1 egg, beaten
100g (4oz) icing sugar
2 tablespoons desiccated coconut
green food colouring
★ adult help

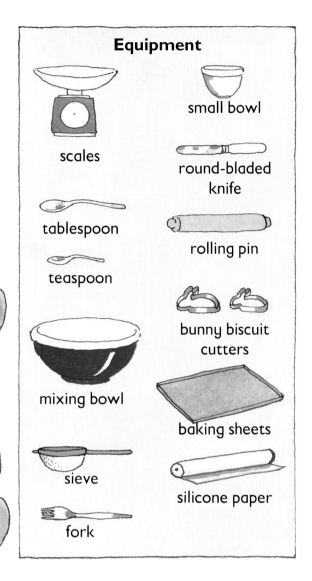

Equipment

scales

small bowl

round-bladed knife

tablespoon

rolling pin

teaspoon

bunny biscuit cutters

mixing bowl

baking sheets

sieve

silicone paper

fork

I cut the margarine into little bits.

It will look like breadcrumbs when it's mixed.

I'm going to stir this well.

I'll sprinkle some flour for you.

1 ▷ Sift the flour, ginger and cinnamon into the mixing bowl. Add the margarine and sugar and rub together with your fingers.

2 ▷ Beat the golden syrup and egg together with a fork, then stir them into the flour mixture and mix until smooth.

Sprinkle the flour onto the work surface and rolling pin and roll out the dough evenly. Using the biscuit cutter cut out 12 bunnies. Roll out the rest of the dough. Divide into 4 flat shapes. Line the baking sheets.

5 Mix the icing sugar with a little water until it is just runny enough to spread. Add a little green colouring to the coconut. Ice the flat bases. Sprinkle over the green coconut then add the bunnies, 3 on each base.

Rolling out pastry

1. Sprinkle flour onto the work surface and rolling pin.
2. Shape the pastry into a ball. Press it flat with the rolling pin.
3. Roll out evenly. Always push the rolling pin away from you. Press on it gently all the time.

Put the bunnies on one baking sheet and the bases on the other. ★Bake the bunnies for 8 minutes and the bases for 12-15 minutes. ★Take out of the oven. When the dough is cool and hard remove from the baking sheets.

Fruit Ices

Choose your favourite juice, add some pretty fruit slices, freeze them and you have a healthy, licky lolly.

You will need

For 4 lollies

lime cordial or fruit juice

small slices of strawberries, apples, cherries, kiwi and mandarin segments

★ adult help

Equipment

jug

4 lolly moulds

lolly sticks

small tray

Mine looks like a flower.

I'm going to use lime now.

2 Arrange the fruit slices in the moulds and very gently pour in the rest of the juice. Put the moulds back in the freezer until completely frozen.

I'm using lime first.

They're yummy!

1 Push the lolly sticks halfway into the moulds. Place the moulds on a tray and half fill them with cordial or juice. Put the moulds in the freezer for 1 hour, or until frozen.

3 Take the lollies out of the freezer, leave for a few minutes, then carefully take them out of the moulds.

Make flavoured ice cubes

Fill the ice tray with lots of different drinks: blackcurrant cordial, orange juice, lime juice, pineapple juice, milk, chocolate milk and even yoghurt. You can add slices of fruit to make it look prettier.

To make ice lollies, cover with cling film. ★Push wooden cocktail sticks or lolly sticks into their centres. The cling film will hold the sticks upright.

Make a huge yoghurt lolly by freezing a pot of your favourite fruit yoghurt. Before you put it in the freezer, push a lolly stick into the centre, through the foil top.

Sparkly Drinks

Here are two drinks you can make for yourself in a few minutes, Fresh Fizzy Lemonade and Witches' Brew, just right to frighten someone on a dark night!

You will need

For the Lemonade

2 lemons

5 tablespoons sugar

2 cups fizzy water

ice cubes

For the Witches' Brew

120ml (4 fl oz) blackcurrant cordial

fizzy water

4 scoops vanilla ice cream

strawberry syrup

Equipment

grater

tablespoon

mixing jug

round-bladed knife

chopping board

ice cream scoop

lemon squeezer

2 glasses for each drink

To make the Lemonade

Mind the lemon pips.

Are you ready yet?

1 Grate about 1 teaspoon of the lemon zest from one of the lemons and put into the jug. Cut each lemon in half and squeeze out the juice. Pour into the jug.

2 Stir the sugar into the juice. Wait until it has dissolved then add the fizzy water.

3 Add the crushed ice and decorate the side of the glass with a slice of lemon and a cherry.

1 Divide the blackcurrant cordial between the two glasses. Pour in the fizzy water.

2 Add 2 scoops of ice cream to each glass. Squeeze over some strawberry syrup and try to drink it before it bubbles over!

Happy Hot Dog

This hot dog is great fun to make but he's so friendly it's almost a shame to eat him.

You will need

1 large hot dog sausage, cooked

1 long bread roll

margarine

ketchup, mayonnaise or mustard

1 cheese slice

2 stuffed olives

1 large pickled cucumber

1 medium pickled cucumber

5cm (2in) slice cucumber

corn or mustard relish

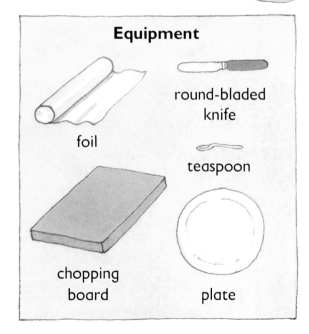

Equipment

foil

round-bladed knife

teaspoon

chopping board

plate

Get everything ready before you begin. Don't forget to wash your hands. Wrap the sausage in foil to keep it warm.

1 Slice the roll about half way along. Push the knife down the middle of the roll, making a hole for the sausage. Spread with margarine.

2 Add ketchup, mayonnaise or mustard and put the sausage inside the roll, leaving a little bit showing for a nose.

3 Cut the cheese slice in half for ear shapes. Fix the ears in place on each side of the sausage.

4 Cut the large pickled cucumber into 4 pieces and use them as legs. Make a slit at the other end of the roll and push in the smaller pickled cucumber for a tail. Press the olives into the roll for eyes.

5 Make the dog's bowl by scooping out the seeds from the middle of the piece of cucumber. Fill it with relish for his dinner.

Ice-box Cake

Here is a cake that you don't bake! All you do is mix the ingredients together, freeze them and hey presto you have a delicious chocolate cake – just ready to slice and eat.

You will need

75g (3oz) butter
25g (1oz) sugar
4 tablespoons cocoa powder
2 tablespoons single cream
50g (2oz) glacé cherries
12 digestive biscuits

Equipment

greaseproof paper

chopping board

450g (1lb) loaf tin

wooden spoon

mixing bowl

round-bladed knife

tablespoon

rolling pin

Get everything ready and weighed out before you begin. Line the tin with greaseproof paper. Cut the glacé cherries in half. **Makes 12 slices**.

1 Soften the butter with the back of your wooden spoon then add the sugar and beat together until light and fluffy. Stir in the cream and cocoa powder and mix until it is smooth and creamy.

2 Put the biscuits between two sheets of greaseproof paper. Crush them with the rolling pin. Leave some quite big pieces as well as crumbs.

Some more ideas

1. You can use the mixture to make crunchy truffles. Roll it into 12 balls, then roll them in chocolate vermicelli and place on a greased baking sheet. Cover with cling wrap before freezing.

3 Mix the crushed biscuits and cherries into the chocolate mixture and spoon it into the lined tin. Cover with more greaseproof paper and place in the freezer for about 3 hours or until the mixture has set.

2. For another tasty version of the cake, use muesli and sultanas instead of the biscuits and cherries.

4 Turn the cake onto a plate, remove the greaseproof paper and leave to thaw for 30 minutes. Cut into 12 slices, or small squares.

Stripy Ice Cream Sundae

See how colourful you can make these huge ice cream sundaes with your favourite flavoured ice cream, jelly and fruit. This recipe uses red and green jelly but you can choose whichever colours you like best.

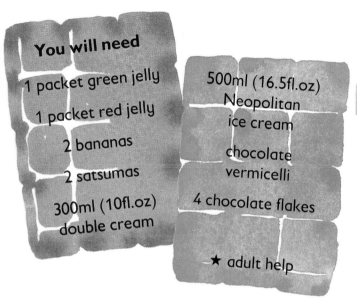

You will need

1 packet green jelly

1 packet red jelly

2 bananas

2 satsumas

300ml (10fl.oz) double cream

500ml (16.5fl.oz) Neopolitan ice cream

chocolate vermicelli

4 chocolate flakes

★ adult help

Equipment

2 bowls

round-ended scissors

measuring jug

1 mixing bowl

ice cream scoop

tablespoon

whisk

round-bladed knife

4 tall ice cream glasses

Get everything ready before you begin.
Makes 4.

1 First of all make the jellies. Follow the instructions on the packets.

2 When the jellies have set, chop them into small pieces. Peel the bananas and satsumas. Slice the bananas and divide the satsumas into segments.

3 ★ Whisk the cream very carefully until it stands in firm peaks. Make sure you don't whisk it too much.

4 Now you can make your ice cream sundaes. Start with a spoonful of red jelly then add some fruit, then a scoop of ice cream. Continue making layers, using a different coloured jelly and ice cream each time until you get to the top. Keep a few slices of banana and satsuma segments to use for decoration.

5 Finish each sundae by covering the top with the whipped cream and decorating it with chocolate vermicelli, fruit and chocolate flake.

Hot chocolate sauce

Here's how to make chocolate sauce to serve with your sundae or with plain ice cream.

All you need is

100g (4oz) plain chocolate

25g (1oz) butter

2 tablespoons milk

1. Break up the chocolate into squares and put them into a pan with the butter and milk.

2. ★ Put the pan over a very low heat and slowly melt the ingredients. Stir all the time with a wooden spoon. You can eat the sauce hot or cold.

Party Time!

Now you are a cook why not have a party for your friends? Here are some ideas for party food you can make yourself.

▶ Make some tiny square sandwiches, just like your Sandwich House on page 8.

Try these fillings:

Sardines mashed with a few drops of lemon juice

Cream cheese with celery and apple slices

Peanut butter and cranberry jelly

▶ Turn your cup cakes into butterflies. Carefully cut a slice off the top. Cut the slice in half. Spread butter icing on top of the cake and stick the two wings in place.

▶ Put pizza toppings on little slices of French loaf. ★Toast them under the grill. Try ham and pineapple, tuna and sweetcorn or sausage and mushroom, on top of the tomato purée and herbs.

▶ Be sure to add your favourite recipe. Serve with your Sparkly Drinks (page 22) and have fun!